JOHN MOLE was born in 1941 in Taunton and now lives in Hertfordshire where for many years he taught in secondary schools and ran The Mandeville Press with Peter Scupham. Recipient of the Gregory and Cholmondeley Awards for poetry, and the Signal Award for his writing for children, he is currently resident poet to the City of London as part of the *Poet in the City* project. He has also published a collection of his review essays as *Passing Judgements* and written the libretto for *Alban*, a community opera which received its première in St Albans Abbey in the spring of 2009.

Poetry

The Love Horse
A Partial Light
Our Ship
From the House Opposite
Feeding the Lake
In and Out of the Apple
Homing
Depending on the Light
Selected Poems
For the Moment
Counting the Chimes: New & Selected Poems 1975–2003
The Other Day
The Bone in Her Leg

For children

Once There Were Dragons
Boo to a Goose
The Mad Parrot's Countdown
Catching the Spider
The Conjuror's Rabbit
Back by Midnight
Hot Air
The Dummy's Dilemma
The Wonder Dish
This is the Blackbird
All the Frogs

Libretto

Alban

Criticism

Passing Judgements: review essays from *Encounter*

Recording

CD from The Poetry Archive: www.poetryarchive.org

To Denise

John Mole

THE POINT
OF LOSS

.... so let the branch be strong

On which you chance to land, a melodious

accidental choice, no giving way

and sing there for the joy of it, the pure joy.

[To a blackbird at first light
John Mole]

ENITHARMON PRESS

With much love

Alan

April, 2014

First published in 2011
by Enitharmon Press
26B Caversham Road
London NW5 2DU

www.enitharmon.co.uk

Distributed in the UK by
Central Books
99 Wallis Road
London E9 5LN

Distributed in the USA and Canada
by Dufour Editions Inc.
PO Box 7, Chester Springs
PA 19425, USA

ISBN: 978-1-907587-04-7

Enitharmon Press gratefully acknowledges the
financial support of Arts Council England.

British Library Cataloguing-in-Publication Data.
A catalogue record for this book is available
from the British Library.

Designed in Albertina by Libanus Press
and printed in England by
Antony Rowe Ltd

For Mary, Margaret and Peter

ACKNOWLEDGEMENTS

Some of the poems in this volume first appeared in the following publications:

The Frogmore Papers, The Interpreter's House, Magma, The North, Poetry Review, The Reader, The Rialto, The Shop, The Spectator, The Times Literary Supplement, and *The War Poetry Review.* Some have also appeared in a limited edition as *The Bone in Her Leg* (Happy Dragons Press, 2008).

CONTENTS

The Point of Loss

GRUFF

How to confront the troll
is head-down, thundering
across a wooden bridge
behind the others
but not looking back.

Be brave, little one,
with your prophet's beard
and dancing feet
whatever rises
from the sullen river.

APPLE ORCHARD

It was too long ago
to be other than Eden
when she called him down
from his father's tree.

So he gathered its fruit
into trouser pockets,
the clasp of his snake-belt
buffed to a shine.

He swung from the branch
which seemed nearest heaven
and ran in to supper
through the last of light.

It was too long ago
to be other than Eden
when he placed on her table
the sun and the moon.

LIKE BONNARD'S WHITE CAT

Everything, with luck,
in working order, wake
like Bonnard's white cat
and for a moment contemplate
the possibility of staying here
exactly where you are
but then, because
at least nine lives are yours,
determine not to let
another minute pass, forget
whatever lies
in wait, surprise
yourself, stretch up
from toe to tip
gigantically grown
and pounce on the unknown.

THE DISTINGUISHED THING

Henry James, dying,
greeted death thus:
Here it is, the distinguished thing.
A lesson for us.

Be prepared, keep
your wit in good nick.
Life may be cheap
but polish the rhetoric.

Never let it show
that you're in a jam.
Get ready to go
with an epigram.

Your birth was undoubtedly
a common affair,
a scowl, a cry
and a gulp of air,

so aim for distinction
this time around,
with Jamesian diction
prepare the ground,

then, no doubting,
as it carries you west,
the distinguished thing
will be impressed.

WHAT COUNTS

Happiness writes against the grain
when every buoyant thought
feels loose and irresponsible
but lights you up. It's enough
that it does, that it goes on
making a world to be at home in,
a various, companionable
celebration of what counts

like walking the dog last thing
for that tug of eagerness
when you step into the dark
calling 'Hey, boy!' and he knows
from habit what comes next
but still strains ahead
as if for the very first time
with a brave new path to follow.

A GAME OF CROQUET

for Orlando Bird

Here in my own childhood's garden
seventeen years ago,
a month before your birth,
your parents came to play a charmed
enchanted game recorded
in this faded snapshot fallen
from a book; your mother's
nimble stateliness, the shadow
of her sunhat on the lawn
between two tilted hoops, your leap
approving father's guile and mischief
when his bold shot touched
and kissed, then both akimbo, leaning
on their mallets, he inquisitive, paternal,
she so intimately sure
that you enjoyed the game, her readiness
and radiant anticipation, knowing you
as if already in her arms.

HEROD REMEMBERS

I dreamed this fox
as red as shame
as it crossed my path
like a lick of flame,

like a cleansing fire-break
sent to divide
the promised land
from a faith that had died,

and the carol it sang
in its immolation
was for every child
of every nation:

I am the offering,
I am the price,
the light of your life
and the sacrifice.

I am the rough beast,
I am the cost
of all you have given,
all you have lost,

and I only tell you
what is and must be
but when you wake
you'll remember me.

I dreamed this fox
as red as shame
and history has taught me
why it came

with its body ablaze,
with its riddling song
as it crossed my path,
looked back, and was gone.

PLAYGROUND

He stands by the wall
unchosen, shifting
from foot to foot,
a bitter nonchalance
to make him invisible.

There is no game
that he cares to join
though plenty
he'd stop in their tracks
if he could.

He is cold stone
near as ice
and nobody's fool,
his toe-caps
tracing circles in the dust

then fixing them
with a kick-start heel
dead centre,
signing off
a zero of oblivion.

When the lunch bell goes
he follows the crowd
at a sullen distance
like a suspect
or an uninvited guest

while the empty playground
behind its railings
and security gate
waits for the laughter
at the end of school.

TO A STUDENT IN THE BALLET MUSEUM

White Lodge, Richmond Park

The hieroglyphs of choreology
are grace notated, step by step
the record of a narrative on staves
strung out across the years
to be loosened into art. These are moves
in search of their full dimension
where a curlicue or circumflex
becomes the body's language
leaping from the page, where beauty
lies in wait for you, your passion,
discipline and hunger for the dance.

Here is the light of the light fantastic,
a balance between rise and fall
that measures its own weight, each pirouette
and lift so accurately written down
along the line, the meticulous transcription
of your gift. This is where you set out
on point from now to curtain call,
to the flower-strewn consummation of applause
when dream and achievement meet
to forget the dull ache in your shoulder
and the running sores on your feet.

Going Blind

She sits at the table where the others sit
but look how differently
she holds her cup and how minutely
different was the way she lifted it

and now there's that distant smile as everyone
gets up and wanders around the house
from room to room, her own pace
that much slower as she follows them.

You might suppose it would be hard to watch
but no. She carries about her such a radiant air
of concentration like a singer
caught up in the music, ready to step on stage

and thrill an audience of thousands, her eyes
as luminous, as dazzlingly bright
as a clear pool's glassy surface
through which the soul prepares for flight.

Die Erblindende

Death's Gift

He knew death's gift, the common knowledge
that life once snatched away there's no retrieving it,
yet when she died, despite his grief, it wasn't rage
he felt against the darkness as she slipped from sight

but an assurance that their love was leased
to unfamiliar possession, all that they were
become translated, giving up its ghost
to join with others in a future they would share.

This was how he stole a march on death
by recognising its community through her,
almost at home already, so that no residual
burden of despair – her suffering, his unbelief –
could touch them as they walked together
making out the way, and all was well.

Der Tod der Geliebten

GHOST

Don't wait up for me again tonight, she said,
the world is large enough already
and I shall be a long while coming home
to this silence you must learn to live with.
So many by-ways, misdirections,
chance encounters before setting out
to discover what we've lost; the stairwell
pounding with eagerness, the apartment
where you made those promises that age
would only make our love the greater,
where, because we both believed them,
separation has become bewilderment
like blindly stumbling down a corridor
to wake up breathless in the dark.

You know that's how it has to be, she said,
vanishing even as he called her back.

LAUNDRY

The precious linen, pleated,
starched and parcelled,
crossed with string,
was dropped off at her door,

brought in, unwrapped
to shine out
from its Jack-and-Jill brown paper
snow on snow

to make an altar
of the kitchen table,
rough hands hesitating
then pressed down
as if a memory of softness
might still rise to hold them
as she seized the bundle,
cradling it, face buried
to absorb the consolation
with a stifled cry,

to thank whatever god
for miracle enough
in such an empty house
at such a time as this
in any season.

JOHN CLARE
Helpston c. 1820

With their golden notebooks
they stop to watch him carting hay;
the embossed enclosures
of the carriages they step from
wait to bear them home.

They'll celebrate the dignity of labour
from safe seats, the prospects
they return to, stable their horses,
hear the harness loosed and jingling
like coins of the realm.

It will have been a profitable day
to do nothing about it, besides
what is there to be done?
Conscience sleeps in the sun,
the poor being always with us.

He watches the future drive off
in its shining hatch-backs
down Heritage Lane
then, seized by love and anger,
takes up his pen to write.

FATHER

Dogged by his collar
the Lord was after them.
They sat at table
heads hung down
with no escape from grace.

They were always about to receive
and truly thankful.
Everything else
apart from gratitude
was his concern not theirs.

THE TRANSFORMATION

Dreaming of walls and spires and splendour rising
with the music of pure thought, the architect
has heard their height and breadth call out
above the traffic's clamour. They sing
with the hope of all that a fresh beginning
will make of his plan, their weight
become a welcome built securely into light
and a future in which each stone takes wing.

He wakes to the business of responsibility
which cannot let him rest. He has begun
to realise his gift in every line he traces
and his vision follows it, a harmony
to echo what in the promise of that dream was sung
until it rises from the city's vacant spaces.

*Written for, and read at, the Poet in the City event 'Poetry and
the Built Environment' (19 February 2008 at the German
Gymnasium, St Pancras)*

WHAT YOU KNOW YOU KNOW

Look down at his feet and consider them
or the bound hands carried in his lap
like a gift for someone else's children.
Not a blink, not a tremor of the lip,
not a word for the world which would
otherwise know him. Interrogate
his silence. It is buried with the dead.
Another sacrifice has claimed its effigy
which sits here beyond how or why
or guilt or innocence or wrong or right.

CANDIDATE

The celebrity make-over of perfect teeth
in a mouth wide open to display them.

Out on the hustings, party-time
and lip-gloss. Dressed to scream

above the frequency of adoration
roaring back. So many faces.

Jacket a mandatory hunting red
to set the state ablaze, a manicure

for the people, singling them out
with startled eyes, her winning finger's

eloquent blood diamond, family values
and the folksiness of God.

CLUEDO

He promised her everything
said the lead piping.

His hypocrisy got on my wick
said the candlestick.

Likewise his superior manner
said the spanner.

He forgot to seal the envelope
said the rope.

She stood and watched him stagger
said the dagger.

Remorse will absolve her
said the revolver.

Which of them did it
if all six admit it?

On the body was found
an ambiguous wound

which to this very day
has had nothing to say.

THE CALL

As the car drives off with a crunch of gravel
and a window blind lifts in an upstairs room
somebody watches the happy couple
then steps back into a spread of gloom.
Whatever the business it isn't finished,
echoes recede from a closing door,
and the light of a life not quenched but diminished
burns as it never dared do before.
Cold meat waits on the kitchen table
to witness the act which must take place soon
then stay where it is for the law's arrival
and the unhappy couple hurrying home.
In an instant their future together has vanished,
at least as they planned it. There on the floor
with the blood still wet in a room still unfurnished
lies a body they can't recognise any more.

Everything here is much as they left it
apart from this horror. No, nothing at all
could have given them either the cause to expect it
or make any sense now, but who made the call?
Did the law know already what it would find?
Right from the start did it have them in mind?
They have always been told they'll live to regret it,
that after the better the worse must befall,
and now, though they've both done their best to forget it,
the writing is finally on the wall.
The vows are exchanged, the register signed,
but a hand at that window has drawn down the blind.

FAREWELL, MY LOVELY
A film noir ballad

I was yours and you were mine
around the block, straight down the line,
but, honey, it's just too close to call
now that the writing's on the wall.

I've split and thrown away the key,
undoubled our indemnity.
What we had was once white hot
but passion cools in a tight spot.

The friendly cop who just dropped by
to chew the fat and apple pie
had something other on his mind.
Both of us know what he could find.

The beach house where we spent that night
sleeps in the moon's adulterous light.
Guilty, shameless, unafraid,
we laid our plans and then got laid.

Tomorrow is another day
and I'm a thousand miles away.
Distance fixes a broken heart.
Death is the car that will not start.

There were thoughts we dared not think
when we fixed your husband's drink.
So that's my story, more or less,
though you'll be telling yours, I guess.

You said I was a heel. I am.
Together we fixed the insurance scam,
both of us in it for the ride,
but our goose is cooked, the fish are fried.

The phonograph plays *Tangerine*.
Life is an empty coke machine.
Your ankle bracelet haunts me still.
If that can't save us nothing will.

DISTANT HORIZONS

were made for the movies, the silhouettes
that pass across them, black on white

in a world of colour, the walking wounded
blindly feeling their way, the dread

recurrent horse-back preacher man
whose shadow howls at the moon

and bides its time, the old tin lizzie
hurrying home for Christmas, the lonely

ranch-hand moving on, the underline
of distances where love and pain

and hope and memory light out
or darken to an instance of regret

that snaps the long-shot into focus
far beyond the gate, the numbered mailbox

and the paperboy whose close-up
is the grin which wears a baseball cap

to reassure that all is well enough
and safe in spite of dancing death

who leads the troupe, his facemask
hooded, out there on the cusp

of earth and air, which then dissolves
to credits, silence, and our solitary selves.

THE GETAWAY

1

On the bed
a suitcase empty
but still open.

The room key's
ball and chain.
Your nightdress.

His passport
handed back
too quickly at the desk.

Look at him
and tell me
do you recognise this man?

2

Your heart is beating
behind bars.
The blinds are down.

That hammering
is neither wind nor rain
but somebody wants in.

He waits outside.
A fine mist
shrouds his face.

You call him by a name
already lost
so who is it that comes?

3

Between the pillow
and his head
an understanding.

Between the mattress
and your thigh
a sheet of ice.

Between his nakedness
and body heat
an absence.

Between your hunger
and his appetite
a shadow line.

4

The car you planned
to leave in
is unregistered.

Its ignition's tick
a flint
that will not catch.

The road ahead
has narrowed
to a vanishing perspective.

The way you came
without him
takes you home.

AS EVIDENCE

At the end of his statement
they asked him
Have you anything to add?

He replied, as they
left the tape running
How long have you got?

In the silence that followed
he rewound the years
as they waited and watched

until with a cry
he arrived at his birth
to be duly cautioned.

Where he came from
was where he went.
The money he saved
was the money he spent.

Everything happened
inside his head.
The books he wrote
were the books he read.

Nothing was good
and nothing was bad.
The chances he took
were the chances he had.

Whether noticed or not
made no difference at all.
The cradle he rocked
was the pram in the hall.

Counting the words
became counting the cost.
The children he loved
were the children he lost.

Remaindered, ignored,
disenchanted, bereft.
The girl who arrived
was the woman who left.

Nobody now
remembers his name
but he goes on writing
just the same.

CHECKPOINT

Berlin 1971

Every lost thing is biding its time
in the lining. It slips between
then and now in a wallet
or in the mind. How could he forget
the girl they found there,
the faded photograph of her
from an earlier life
who was not his wife
but, as he stood his ground
in that cold compound
and they made of their interrogation
an intimate humiliation,
gazed at him with a love
which seemed warmth enough?

And how could I not recall
how he told it, death pale
after they'd let him out at last
to rejoin us? What had been worst
he said, was neither the fear
nor reckoning the danger
he was in, but the shame
of not remembering her name
when they gave the photograph back
and he couldn't believe his luck.

IAGO AT LARGE

The only answer that any practical joker can
give to the question 'Why did you do this?' is
Iago's: 'Demand me nothing. What you know,
you know.' W.H. Auden: *The Joker in the Pack*

This one's for you
but the joke is on me,
the cryptic clue,
the duplicate key,

the invisible ink,
the exploding cigar,
the ubiquitous stink
wherever you are,

the flatulent cushion,
the squirting lapel,
not one second's remission
from hurting like hell,

the powder that itches,
the blackfacing soap,
the coven of witches
who toy with your hope,

the rubbery spider,
the Hallowe'en mask,
the headless rider,
the poisoned cask,

the collateral damage,
the specious excuse,
the familiar outrage,
short-lived but profuse,

the innocent witness,
the unwilling recruit,
the blood on the bride's dress,
the stain on your suit.

You may be elsewhere
but here's where I am,
a serious joker
proclaiming the man.

My sport is a riddle
that stands where you fall,
the ending, the middle,
and start of it all.

AUTUMNAL

What he left lay pressed in his back pocket,
a secret, a keepsake, but so familiar
he'd forgotten that it was there. Another year
spun round with its daily business
and promises seemed good as new
except that because he took them for granted
the weather changed, a fresh wind
reminding him in time what life was up to.

And what she found was the linen folded
in a bottom drawer, so feather-weight
it fell into her arms, a drift of snow
already melting. How could she not remember
how things had been before temperate love
packed them carefully away? And now
not a moment too soon she had lifted up the sun
to its full height, dancing the length of her.

QUIET STONES

He brought them back home
from a garden in Kyoto,
the quiet stones, and made a ring
outside their kitchen
to catch the dying light
on summer party evenings.

His wife had her foolproof way
to silence him, his loud
outrageous remarks too much
the life and soul. *Mike,*
you're impossible. Go on
like this and I'll leave you.

Then we'd all erupt
with wild western laughter,
raising a glass to fellowship
and being together
for as long as it would last
which held until now.

The sun rises in the east
because it must this morning
on an English garden
where his stones lie
as he left them, and his wife
is burdened by the quiet.

FINE AND MELLOW

Settled on the stool reserved for her among
this press of jazzmen in a TV studio,
these horns and hats and jackets, Billie Holiday
united one last time with Lester Young
is listening to the instrumental intro,
nodding, smiling, feeling her way.

Love being just around the corner
she bends the words, sends them ahead
then calls them back. What they'll have seen
is already more than enough for her
but not for the song. Life that has made her bed
makes music. Perfection treats us mean.

God bless the child that has her own
and leaves us with it. Listen. Heartbreak
is all in the timing, a fraction behind the beat
turns suffering to joy, to be alone
yet know exactly how a song can make
even the saddest shadow tap its feet.

And as for Lester, risen like a wraith
returning from her past, his fragile chorus
shines in her eyes. Never more at one
than now, the two of them are keeping faith
with all that this music means to us
and all with ears to hear it still to come.

CASTLES

We built our castles on the sand.
The tide came in, and there an end.

We built our castles out of fear.
Trust began to disappear.

We built our castles stone by stone.
Their shadow chilled us to the bone.

We built our castles far apart.
Twin halves of a broken heart.

We built our castles thoughtlessly.
No chance for you, no luck for me.

We built our castles in the air.
Nothing we hoped to find was there.

We built our castles. Let them fall.
Time disposes. Love is all.

THEIR MARRIAGE

He says: If I threw the ball a dog would run after it
wherever we were. That's what dogs do
without question. Balls are for bringing back
between bared teeth fixed in a grin. A dog knows
there's a point to this but not what it is. Also
that your command to sit is worth the whistle,
that something good may come of it. A dog
is not inclined to beg or differ
without reckoning the odds, whether
to take the ball again and run to someone else
or out of habit drop it at your feet.

She says: Since none of this applies to cats
we're wasting time. A cat will either come or go
wherever life serves best to make a home of it.
Look into those eyes which close then open
on a mind made up to stay exactly where it is
and make a virtue of indifference, nothing
to chase or be retrieved except by choice, no
leaping up, no rolling over to be praised.
A dog may take the ball and run with it; a cat
will either rub herself against your naked feet
or pounce to bite them.

A SNOWMAN

They built a snowman out of the coldness of their hearts
not of the air or the flakes or of anything
in between. It was a laying on of frozen hands,
a remedial sculpture they could almost
wrap their arms around. The children watched
from their bedroom window, finding no sense
in what they saw, two penitents with a world
to reclaim which wasn't working, a palpable
confusion, mother, father, and whatever else.

Then overnight the thaw began, and spread itself
across a lawn of darkness. What remained
was a monumental patience, the last
blocked ice to disappear. The children
wondered at its gradual melting,
wrapped up warm and went out in the sun.

BERRIES

Thrusting my stained hand
through a veil of dew
at sunrise, keeping the promise
made last night
to bring them back for you,
I think of your fingers
on my lips last thing
before we fell asleep
and how I slipped from bed
like a thief this morning.

TO A BLACKBIRD AT FIRST LIGHT

Clasp whatever branch you may land on
and, just for the joy of it, from a full throat
sing, before flight, of yet another season
coming into leaf. Let every grace note
seed where it falls, and the point-blank
not-to-be-born-again remorselessness of dawn
receive your gift. As if there were God to thank
for this, as if not randomly thrown
but scattered for a purpose, may your song
resist interpretation much as beauty does
the suffering it causes. So let the branch be strong
on which you chance to land, a melodious
accidental choice, no giving way,
and sing there for the joy of it, the pure joy.

THE LEGEND
Hallsands

We visited, to be spooked
by ghostliness, a coastal village
emptied, echoing,
left behind: its stone hotel's
bay windows, sea-green
Lloyd Loom painted chairs,
the glass-topped table,
even a magazine left open
facing down
as if to mark the place
and hide a secret. Nobody else
it seemed had come or gone
that August afternoon except
the two of us and our newborn
sleeping in his pram.
You wore your mini sundress
with the knotted straps
I'd hurry to undo
back on the narrow bed
in our fortnight-rented cottage
as we'd make fresh love
and out of such happiness
our own unclouded legend.

What haunts me now
about this memory, this
sudden visitation of a past
from more than thirty years,
is how it seems that those chairs
were waiting for us
as they yawned at emptiness,
the magazine knew

how the story went,
and the table's glass-top
was the looking glass
we must all walk through
in the end. I see us
sitting there, and wonder
whether we're alone
or whether at any moment
passing by outside
and looking up, a couple
with their first child
starting out on life
as we were then, our own ghosts
passionate in summer heat,
might still remember
where the cottage was
and take the inland road there
hurrying back.

AFTER RAIN

Walking around the block
to shrug off weariness
and notice perhaps
how a letterbox shines
or gutters drip,

how the fishbone skeleton
of an aerial swims
in a clear sky
and a doorstep cat
has resumed its watch,

is to come back
into language, the promise
of finding words
for company
and what the sun can do.

THE WATER'S EDGE

On this flat hard shine
we rehearse unsteadiness,
a buffeted progress
through thin rain.

With a shrug of impatience
you lean on my arm
and drag it down,
recalling how once

we lay together
as the tide washed in
then broke from loving
to chase each other.

How it is now
is what must be,
strange, unsteady
and cold, although

here where we walk
this flat hard shine
still holds our reflection
against the dark.

THE VILLAGE ROAD

for Bob and Margaret Grover

What is that dark enclosing shade
drawn down across the hill?
Is it the agitation of a storm
as rain clouds start to fill?

No. It is Death's arrival.
He rides by the light of day
with a shadowy host for company
and cannot stop or stay.

Young lovers run ahead of him
in all their prime and pride
while the fresh babes on his saddle
are lined up side by side.

The old cry out for mercy,
the young ones beg for time:
Oh let us go by the village road,
take a last look at home.

Let us stop beside the brook
to drink and draw our breath
so that we may remember
the kindliness of Death.

But Death in his compassion
knows about grief and pain:
We must avoid the village.
You cannot go there again.

Every wife and mother,
father, daughter, son,
would cling so close their love knot
could never be undone.

After A.N. Maikov and Rosa Newmarch

GHOSTS

It's a habit of theirs
to arrive unbidden
as they were in life,
in the full flush of it.
How they choose the moment
with an antique courtesy
about their business:
*May we step aside
and speak with you alone?*

They have so much
to ask, so little time
before the cock crows
but we share it out
between us, theirs
being dearly bought
and paid back
by the minute, mine
whatever is allowed.

Do I remember
the cracked cup, the privet
and laburnum, that climb
up Dunkery, the run
down Porlock Hill
in neutral, the explosive
fizz of Tizer, Endicott's
corner shop, how Maggie
disappeared and why?

Had they imagined
that I should still be here
and older than them all
to tell them Yes, that few things
matter more to me
than keeping faith
with what returns like this,
reclaiming it in celebration
at the point of loss?

So we impart a portion
of the secret held
between us, fading back
together, each of them
to where the past still waits
for who they were, while I
already watch my own ghost
step aside in readiness
for what I shall become.

ALL FOR LOVE
c. 1960

Not how to spend this summer afternoon
with the window closed, a borrowed LP's
vinyl warped to a wheel-wobble,
secretly in my college room, the turn-table
lurching through *Teach Yourself Ballroom*.

Behind the door a dinner-jacket
lynched on its hanger, those sad lapels
a study in dejection. Plus a clip-on
burgundy bow tie, a matching
cummerbund and, oh my God, the pumps.

The threat of it, that such equipment
should conspire to make a man of me
or dress my shame, and all for the quick quick
slow of saxophone and violin,
strict tempo, mapping the landscape

step by step, a combat manual's tracery
of angled footprints. Over the top
tomorrow night, but as for now
just one more time alone, and holding close
romance's nemesis in rigid arms.

THE ISLAND

Out there, that immanent
speck on the horizon,
a day's journey or less
drawn homeward
entering the house I left,
then risen to meet me
my father from his chair
through clouds of pipe-smoke

where all I can make out
are wisdom and loneliness,
rugs on the carpet,
his tartan slippers
and a tall lamp standing
in its pool of light.

THE BONE IN HER LEG

For my dear aunt,
theatrically arthritic,
who went about
with a bone in her leg,
it was growing old
before her time
and letting us know it
that kept her young.

She practised the art
of an ancient mischief
which searched out laughter
in every complaint.
It never took long
and as soon as she found it
pain shed gold dust
under her feet.

When she took to the grave
at the end of all,
as she might have said
like a duck to water,
the bone in her leg
stood up and applauded
then lay back down
where she told it to.

UNCLE STAN'S CHRISTMAS

No need to ask him why –
this was his winter of profound content,
waistcoat unbuttoned, kipper tie
bouncing with merriment.

Laughter, quick and explosive
from the arm-chair's deep-sunk
trench to wallow in. *May we all live
for ever!* he roared. Drunk,

I suppose, looking back,
or just plain loudly grateful.
*Knick knack paddywhack,
give the dog another plate-full.*

Then after supper, he drove the piano
one-handed, cut-glass whiskey
topped up, ready to go
beside him, and our lit tree

rocking to his abandon, hell
for leather, four beats to the bar,
with its fairy-lights, its angel
and its cold five-pointed star.

GOOD FOR BUSINESS

The sidesman at our church was Mr Fear,
appropriately named despite the grin
he'd greet the congregation with, his thin
moustache, his dapper dandy-ish good cheer.
Appropriate, that is, because his trade
was funeral direction. What's in a name
can be adapted, though. That very same
eponymous coincidence he made
doubly profitable by reversing it
and adding to his parlour's sign outside
a second occupation, not as safe
or grounded as the first, but showing wit
as well as versatility. A bride,
a groom, and wedding photographs by Raef.

A TOAST TO MOUSTACHES

Had Lloyd George known my father
they might have compared moustaches
proud of a proliferating bush
like Elgar's or Conan Doyle's.
Did they too comb theirs every morning
admiring the walrus in the mirror
which basked on an upper lip
as they sang the song of Empire?
Or was it the unwaxed topiary
of an English country garden
meticulously trimmed to effect?
Not for such as them the spiv's twig
thin as a stocking seam, its circumflex
above a smile with pointed teeth,
and definitely not the appliqué
of a Belgian detective in its hairnet
shrouded overnight. Better the unkempt
scholar's hedgerow, its frizzle
of absentmindedness, than tyranny's
clipped imitation of a clerk.
Never the twin shoots of the fencing master
spiked at both ends, but nothing less
than a trusty growth was good for business
in the boardroom of the family firm.
So celebrate the hirsute
in its place, in the land of our fathers
with the pipes and trouser presses,
waistcoats and hunters, ashplants
and buttoned gloves, for who would be
clean-shaven in that company
and not compare moustaches,
how best to cut a dash, to patronise
the photographic studio, or gallantly
to brush against a favoured lady's hand.

THOSE LOVELY OLD WAR PEOPLE

I stood beside her
at his memorial service
and the interment
of a hero's ashes.

He had known her father,
and the congregation
out-ranking us
was of another age.

We stood around the grave
among so many medals
and a pride of regimental colours
fallen silent.

Then, as we walked away,
she chirruped
Aren't they wonderful,
these lovely old war people?

With such unselfconsciousness
and almost breaking into song
she could have passed
for a force's sweetheart.

Her hair no longer quite
as I remembered it
with ash-grey flecks
among the gold.

Well she said,
you know what I mean,
and how can I help
not think of daddy?

GRACE AND FAVOUR

The shop bell's
whanging coil, their entry's
imprimatur, boxed
provisions carried for them
to the boot: We'll settle up
next week if that's
acceptable. The cost of everything.
I've found a little man
who doesn't overcharge . . .

We grew to judgement
by the names our mothers
gave them. *Mr or Mrs*
so and so who'd got
above themselves, although
they practised charity
and sat in church.
This was our inheritance
of grace and favour,
the old bitch gossip
and small kindnesses.

THE BICYCLE BOYS

c. 1910

No helmet, no lycra,
but rough tweed and Elgar,

solitary chaps
with their trouser clips,

their books of verse,
their pipes, of course,

and their bottled ale
for body and soul,

they followed their dreams
along hilltop lanes

or stopped to read
in a patch of shade

as the clouds passed over
for now and ever

and time lay still
like a ticking wheel

which spun to its rest
in the wayside grass,

but then home before dark
for tomorrow's work

at the office desk,
the quotidian task,

the weekend done,
the downhill run

as free as air,
and each handlebar

the boss's gripped throat
as like as not.

THE ALLOTMENT
for Chris and Liz Rolfe

How much of earth
is allowed, how
much time on it

to plant, to cultivate,
dig deep
and watch what

rises from the dark
to meet us
with its annual

display, another
miracle on
lease, each year

more precious
as the seasons
turn, return

until the mystery
of our birth
is bedded down.

SPARROWS AND BAMBOO

A Japanese miniature

If one should take off
before the other
with a flick of the wing
or a tail feather,

if the song should remain
because incomplete
when both have flown
and are out of sight,

if we should find words
to remember it by
but then forget
the melody,

observe this silent
speckled pair
and the music they print
on a sheet of air.

WHERE WE CAME IN

This is where we came in, remember,
when the screen was a close-up kiss
and the back row beckoned, when love
for the price of a ticket tried it on
with my hand in yours, when this
was as far as we went, our faces
turned to the flickering print of light
like pale moths eager to be burned.

And so we were, in the flames
of a tumescent music, ready
for the next time round. No news
or second feature held a candle
to the main attraction as we stood there
shining in the rain, then sailed
a dreamboat home to nakedness
which was where we came in, remember.

Tailpieces

LITTLE JOHN RUSKIN
(Praeterita)

He stared at the patterns in his room
until they mapped an intimate cartography
to become the world, and soon
he found himself an aesthete by the age of three
when, taken to have his portrait done
at Mr Northcote's studio, it was a hole
he noticed in the carpet troubled him
as if it had designs upon his soul.

WESSEX

Then Wessex came in again. I asked if Hardy could
stroke him. So he bent down and stroked him like the
master of the house. Wessex went on wheezing away.
Virginia Woolf, Diaries, 25 July 1926

Stroked at the request
of yet another persistent guest,

he knew that his reputation
was for halting a conversation

which had come too close to the bone,
Please go, please leave us alone.

So whoever it was this time
would be offered no reason or rhyme

by a poet with nothing to say
and an old dog wheezing away.

WHAT THE POET TOLD ME

Keep the pot at a quiet simmer,
Be there for the lightning strike,
Coax a gleam from a glimmer,
Go easy with *as* and *like*.
Don't over-extend the metaphor,
Take care to drop it in time,
And your poem will be all the better for
Avoiding the obvious rhyme.
Never call it poetic licence
When a line is arcane or obscure –
To say 'Your sense just isn't my sense'
Is the mark of an amateur.
Beware that windy inflation
Which bicycle pumps the heart
And the gilded illumination
Of the capital A of Art.
Cut down on the definite article
Make the personal pronoun think twice,
Be rigorous, ruthless, self-critical
And free to reject this advice.

MOTHER WOULDN'T LIKE IT

I dreamed I met Auden shuffling through the snow
in a shapeless overcoat on Fifth Avenue.

His devoted reader, I took a dim view
of his looking so shabby and told him so.

'My dear' he replied, 'it's the best I can manage'
which abruptly ended our conversation

as he disappeared into the subway station
and I woke to find myself on a blank page.

PROFESSIONAL

There's something about endurance
which marks the passing of time
in ways you might never expect.
What, for example, as he waited
for help, was all Cole Porter could do,
both legs crushed beneath his fallen horse?

No future now to be counted on
beside the reckoning of pain, he lay there
rhyming, gripped by a melody,
and added verses to another love song
millions would dance to, each phrase
able-bodied, getting the metre right.

THE LINGO

Exchanging the humdrum for what I was not
like fronting the band in a white tuxedo
and all the dancers loving my tempo
was giving my fantasy all I'd got.

To be Fred to Ginger without rehearsal,
lifting her six feet in the air.
'Oh boy!' she'd exclaim. 'Take me anywhere.
You're top of the world, you're a natural.'

To go where I'd get without much practice
or any at all if the going was good,
speaking the lingo my dreams understood –
'Make mine a highball with plenty of ice.'

STROKING THE FUR BACKWARDS

Not to sit there with the cat on your knee,
being already elderly
and reassuring yourself
as the flat of your hand passes over
that what is must always be,

but to stroke the fur backwards
with deliberate intent
so that from this false controlling element
you might both leap free.